Ill health can so easily ruin a carefully planned, eagerly anticipated, holiday or business trip.

How often have you been laid low by a tummy bug or the effects of sunburn? Yet most of these problems can be avoided with a little care, commonsense, basic knowledge, and forward planning.

'HAVE A GOOD TRIP!' aims to tell you what you need to know to protect your health when you travel at home and abroad, and so get the best out of your trip.

'HAVE A GOOD TRIP!' is endorsed by the Health Education Council, and contains concise and essential information ranging from recommended vaccinations and the insurance to look for, to how to cope with sunburn and diarrhoea.

A comprehensive packing checklist is also included together with sections on fitness, first-aid, how to 'phone home in an emergency from all the popular overseas destinations, metric conversion tables, and a list of foreign words you will find useful.

In other words this pocket sized book will help you to . . .

HAVE A GOOD TRIP!

Have A Good Trip! The Travel Health Guide
© 1984 Brian O'Boyle

First Published in 1983 by
Micropharm Ltd., Morshead Road, London W9 1LF

Second edition 1984
Third edition 1984

Printed in Great Britain by
Cox & Wyman Ltd., Reading, Berks.

Art Direction Brian O'Boyle
Cover illustration and cartoons by Kim Outram
Graphic Design Allen Greenall Dip.A.D., LSIA
Typeset by PRG TypoGraphics Ltd., Cheddar, Somerset

ISBN 0 9509290 0 X

Designed and Published by
MICROPHARM LTD
London, England

HAVE A GOOD TRIP!

The Travel Health Guide

By Brian O'Boyle B.Sc. M.P.S.

**MICROPHARM
LONDON**

Acknowledgements

I am very grateful to the following people and organisations for comments and material received:

British Airways; The British Insurance Association; Th British Red Cross Society; British Telecom; The Dept. Health and Social Security; Europ Assistance; The Health Education Council; The International Associat for Medical Assistance to Travellers; The Ministry of Agriculture Fisheries and Food; P.J. O'Boyle F.R.C.S.; Dr. E.M. O'Boyle; The Pharmaceutical Society of Gre Britain; RADAR; I.J. Swann F.R.C.S.; Domenico Tellatin Thomas Cook; The World Health Organisation.

. . . and my wife Barbara, for her endless patience and understanding.

PREFACE TO THE THIRD EDITION

The first edition of 'HAVE A GOOD TRIP!', published June 1983, received remarkably good reviews in many national newspapers including The Daily Express, The Times, The Yorkshire Post, The Glasgow Herald, The Sunday Post, and The Sunday Express. It was also recommended on the BBC travel and leisure radio programme Breakaway, and by Michael Aspell on Capital Radio.

Most readers typically commented that it was 'useful', 'interesting', 'informative', and 'helpful'.

Encouraged by these reactions, the text was expanded to take into account expert technical comments received, and a revised booklet was published in January 1984 as a special edition for a major travel company.

This, the third pocket sized edition, contains several new sections, and aims to answer most of your holiday healthcare questions in simple everyday language.

Brian O'Boy

London 1984

CONTENTS

PACKING CHECKLIST

Use this Checklist when packing.
Pick and choose to suit your trip.

THE THINGS YOU MUSTN'T FORGET Tick

Tickets...☐
Passport and Visas...☐
Vaccination Certificates...☐
Foreign Cash...☐
Traveller's Cheques..☐
Chequebook and Cheque Card (Eurocheque Card)..................☐
Credit Cards...☐
Some Sterling for your return...☐
Health Insurance Policy and Certificate...................................☐
DHSS Form E111 and Leaflets SA30 and SA36*.......................☐
Car: International Driving Licence or Permit/Bail Bond for Spain..☐
Vehicle Registration Documents/Licence/MOT/GB Plate.............☐
Vehicle Insurance and 'Green Card Extension'..........................☐
First-Aid Kit/Fire Extinguisher/Warning Triangle.......................☐
Spares Kit (bulbs; fan belt; hoses etc.) Emergency Windscreen....☐
Cancel the deliveries – milk, papers, bread etc........................☐
Turn off the Water/Gas/Electricity (except Freezer)..................☐
Ask the Neighbours/Police to Keep an Eye on Your Home............☐
Lock all Doors and Windows and Move Plants from Window-sills..☐

SOME OF THE THINGS YOU ALMOST ALWAYS FORGET
Alarm Clock...☐
Camera/Films/Flashgun/Batteries...☐
Corkscrew/Bottle Opener/Can Opener......................................☐
Contact Lenses and/or Spectacles...☐
Dentures (Spare)!...☐
Detergent for Washing Clothes...☐
Hair Dryer..☐
International Electrical Adaptor...☐
Iron for Clothes..☐
Nail Clippers/File/Scissors...☐
Passport Photos (for ski passes etc.).......................................☐
Penknife...☐
Pocket Dictionary/Phrase Book..☐
Sewing Kit...☐
Shoe Polishing Kit..☐
Sunglasses..☐
Swimwear..☐
Toilet Bag..☐
Torch...☐

*for reciprocal healthcare arrangements – see "Insurance"

8

OTHER PHARMACY AND HEALTH CARE ITEMS YOU MIGHT NEED

	Tick
A supply of your **personal medicines** labelled with the **unbranded name** (not just the **brand name**) and the **dosage**	☐
Anti-diarrhoeal Tablets or Mixture	☐
Antihistamine Cream/Spray/Tablets	☐
Anti-malarial Tablets	☐
Calamine containing Lotion	☐
Cleansing Cream/Lotion	☐
Cold Cream	☐
Contraceptives	☐
Crepe Bandage	☐
Dental Floss	☐
Glucose and Electrolyte Mixture for Dehydration	☐
Hand Cream	☐
Indigestion Tablets	☐
Insect Repellant/Insecticidal Spray	☐
Laxative Tablets	☐
Lip Salve	☐
Medicated Foot Powder/Cream	☐
Moisturising Cream/Lotion	☐
Mouth Wash	☐
Pain Relief Tablets	☐
Shampoo	☐
Soap	☐
Sterile Wound Dressing	☐
Throat Lozenges	☐
Toilet Paper	☐
Tooth Brush/Toothpaste	☐
Total Sunblock for Lips	☐
Travel Sickness Tablets	☐
Tweezers	☐
Triangular Bandage	☐
Water Purification Tablets	☐
Water Resistant Sunscreen	☐

YOUR FIRST-AID KIT

First-Aid Guidance Leaflet	☐
Absorbent Lint BPC 15g	☐
Antiseptic Cream 15g	☐
Antiseptic Wipes	☐
Assorted Waterproof Plasters	☐
Cotton Wool 15g	☐
Open Wove Bandage 5cm	☐
Paracetamol Tablets	☐
Safety Pins	☐
Scissors	☐
Zinc Oxide Tape 2·5cm	☐

FIGHT THE FLAB
ARE **YOU** FIT FOR YOUR TRIP?

This guide tells you how to protect your health when you travel at home or abroad, but how healthy are you right now, and how much do you know about looking after yourself?

Quiz

This quick quiz may give you a few surprises! Tick one choice for each question and check the answers at the end.

1. Apart from feeling better and fitter, what is the main benefit of regular exercise?
   A. It tones up your complexion.
   B. It gives you a healthy appetite.
   C. It helps your heart and arteries stay younger longer.

2. Regular exercise can build up your strength, develop your stamina and keep you supple. Which is most important for protecting your heart?
   A. Strength.
   B. Stamina.
   C. Suppleness.

3. Which is the best indication that the exercise you are doing is helping to build up stamina?
   A. It makes you sweat a lot.
   B. It makes you slightly breathless.
   C. It makes your muscles ache a little.

4. Here are three forms of exercise. Assuming you do it regularly, which one is best for developing stamina?
   A. Vigorous swimming.
   B. Yoga.
   C. Weight-lifting.

5. Which of the following is the average Briton eating too much of?
   A. Fatty food.
   B. Frozen vegetables.
   C. Breakfast cereals.

6. Which of the following is the average Briton not eating enough of?
   A. Protein.
   B. Vitamins.
   C. Roughage.

7. Which of the following foods is most fattening?
   A. Wholemeal bread.
   B. Jacket potatoes.
   C. Salted peanuts.

8. Apart from looking and feeling better, what is the main benefit of staying slim?
   A. You can eat bigger meals.
   B. You can think faster.
   C. It helps your heart and arteries stay younger longer.

Answers

1. C Helps avoid heart attacks and strokes.
2. B Improves the efficiency of your circulation.
3. B Because your heart and lungs are being well-exercised.
4. A Dynamic exercise using large muscles.
5. A High in calories, and may be linked to heart disease.
6. C Prevents constipation and has other health benefits.
7. C Nearly three times as many calories as wholemeal bread.
8. C Helps avoid heart attacks and high blood pressure.

The Vital S-Factors

True physical fitness is something more than simply being fit to cope with the stresses and strains of everyday life. It means possessing 3 important qualities – SUPPLENESS, STRENGTH and STAMINA – the vital S-factors.

S for Suppleness

First, suppleness, or flexibility. Neck, spine and joints should be developed to move freely, thus reducing the risk of sprained ligaments or pulled muscles and tendons. The more supple you are, the less likely you are to suffer aches and pains brought on by stiffness.

S for Strength

Next, strength. That's extra muscle-power in reserve for those often unexpected heavier jobs. Lifting and shifting need strong shoulder, trunk and thigh muscles. Toned-up tummy muscles also help to take the strain . . . and keep your waistline trim.

S for Stamina

Finally stamina. This is staying power, endurance, the ability to keep going without gasping for breath. For stamina, you need good blood circulation through a healthy heart and well tuned muscles so that plenty of vital oxygen gets to where it's needed. With stamina, you have a slower, more powerful heartbeat. You can cope more easily with prolonged, or heavy exertion, and you'll be less likely to suffer from heart disease.

So How Fit Are You?

The best tests of fitness are those that measure STAMINA and involve rhythmic movement of large groups of muscles for sustained periods.

Test 1. Try walking up and down a flight of stairs (about 15 steps) THREE times fairly briskly. You should be able to hold an ordinary conversation without being at all out of breath.

Test 2. Run on the spot. Lift your feet at least 6 inches off the floor. Keep going until you feel a bit short of breath or tired, then stop. If you're over 50 you should be able to manage TWO minutes. Younger people should find THREE minutes quite easy.

Benefits And Bonuses Of Exercise

For some people, games at school were hell! While the 'enthusiasts' ran, jumped and enjoyed themselves, the rest lurked in the locker room or enjoyed a crafty cigarette in the bicycle shed. But as people get older, perspective changes, and the sport you choose to take part in is much more fun than the one you're forced into. In addition, sporting activity brings you into contact with like minded people, so the relaxation afterwards is just as important as the exercise.

But what good does taking exercise actually do you?

1. Exercise improves the staying power of your heart and circulation and may protect against coronary heart disease.
2. It keeps your neck, back and joints supple and your posture right.
3. It tightens flabby muscles and gives you strength.
4. It helps you stay slim.
5. It helps combat stress.
6. It can be great fun.
7. It helps you feel good in mind and body.

What Form Of Exercise Is Best?

Essentially, exercise that builds up stamina, or staying power. Top of the list are swimming, cycling, jogging and rowing, all things you can do on holiday as well as at home. Disco dancing is good too, but remember if you are not used to taking exercise, you should **start gradually and build up slowly and consult your doctor before you start (even before you do the above tests), if you have been ill, or suffer from any complaint.**

Swimming is just about the best all-round form of exercise there is, ideal for developing all three S-Factors – stamina, suppleness and strength. It makes you feel fresher and fitter and is ideal for getting you started on a fitness routine.

Because your body is supported by the water, your spine and joints can move freely, and it's a load off your back, hips, knees and feet. This makes swimming a superb form of exercise for everyone, young and old, and particularly those with back trouble, arthritis or rheumatism.

Squash is probably the fastest and best racquet game for fitness, but you must be fit before you take it up. Like squash, **badminton** is an indoor game and so can be played all the year round. Both badminton and **tennis** are stop-start games, so to get maximum fitness benefit, both partners must try to keep rallies going and play hard.

14

Team sports have the benefit of giving people the push they need to train regularly, and regular exercise is what most of them need. With some games such as football and rugby, players make quick short bursts, putting pressure on the heart and circulation and make heavy demands on certain groups of muscles. With basketball, or netball on the other hand, players are moving for much of the time, and are much more active. Where you play in a team is important – hockey goalkeepers, for example, are much less active than forwards.

While team games are obviously unappealing to middle-aged people, swimming, badminton, and tennis can provide useful forms of exercise. **Golf** is not particularly good for fitness, but it is certainly relaxing and gets you out into the open air. Walking briskly has benefits for health and swinging a club keeps you supple.

Jogging, like all the best forms of exercise, has the two essential ingredients – it improves the staying power of your heart and lungs. You'll get most benefit if you jog every day, but every other day is often enough. LESS OFTEN, AND YOU LOSE THE TRAINING EFFECT. Jogging is running free and easy, at a comfortable trot. There's no urgency, no strain, no competition.

Build up gradually over a period of six weeks to a final session of at least ten and preferably twenty minutes. Don't jog within two hours of your last meal, if you feel tired or weak, if you have a cold or feel one coming on, and an obvious safety precaution, when it's foggy.

Track suits made of natural fibre, such as cotton, are best for jogging, and light-coloured kit or a reflector jacket are essential if you plan to jog at night. It's also vital to wear the right shoes with thick rubber insoles and good arch support.

Warming Up

BEFORE any vigorous exercise, it is wise to spend two or three minutes limbering up, with a series of simple stretching exercises. This not only helps to keep your joints fully flexible, but also tones up all your major muscle groups.

Here are five easy stretching movements. Repeat each movement slowly **10 times,** without overdoing it – and breathing normally throughout, there's no hurry.

1. **Head rolling.** Stand with your feet apart and hands on hips. Tip your head back and look straight up at the ceiling. Roll your head slowly round to face the right, then the floor, then the left, and finally the ceiling again. Repeat in the other direction.

2. **Side bending.** With feet still apart and hands on your sides, lean first to the right, straight up again, and then lean to the left, sliding the hand down the side of the leg each time.

3. **Arm swinging.** Still standing feet apart, push both arms out straight in front of you, fingertips touching. Raise them above your head then down to your sides pushing each arm backwards at the same time.

4. **Trunk twisting.** Stand feet apart with your hands straight out in front of you, fix your eyes on your right hand and swing your arm round to the right, keeping it straight, as far as it will go. Repeat the whole movement with the left arm.

5. **Hip flexing.** Stand feet together. Bring one knee up to your chest, pulling it with your hands if necessary. Then bow your head and touch your knee with your forehead. Repeat with the other knee.

You Are What You Eat!

Exercise is only one part of a fitness package. Eating for health is just as important. The main thing is to have a balanced diet, which means eating fresh fruit and vegetables, fish and poultry, cutting down on fatty and fried food and reducing your sugar intake.

Balance is the key word, and the one form of food you are possibly not getting enough of is **fibre.**

Fibre is found only in the cell walls of plants. So obviously, meat, poultry, eggs, fish, and dairy products, the things we eat most of, contain no fibre at all.

Fibre does a lot more for your health than simply provide 'roughage' to prevent constipation – though this is important enough. Lack of fibre seems to be connected with various other disorders of the bowels, including piles, and a serious inflammation called diverticulitis.

What's more, if you are worried about your waistline, eating more fibre may actually help you stay slim! Food with plenty of fibre like potatoes or bread, are bulky. They can satisfy your hunger without loading your body with calories. The fatty and sugary things we eat so much of today are just the opposite. That's why so many people have a weight problem. And if you are overweight, you run a greater risk of heart disease.

High fibre foods include baked beans, bran cereal, peas, wholemeal bread, sweetcorn, jacket potatoes, wholewheat pasta, lentils, and baked apples.

Combine HIGH FIBRE FOODS with HEALTHY EXERCISE and in a few weeks you won't recognise yourself – you'll be in great shape to get the most out of your trip!

For more detailed advice on how to get fit for your holiday and stay fit when you return, write for a FREE "Looking After Yourself!" booklet to the Health Education Council, 78 New Oxford Street, London WC1A 1AH.

17

VACCINATIONS AND PRECAUTIONS
PLAN WELL AHEAD

Broadly speaking, if you are going anywhere
OUTSIDE NORTHERN EUROPE, NORTH
AMERICA, AUSTRALIA and NEW ZEALAND, you
would be advised to take some kind of
immunisation and health protection.

Europe

FRANCE, SPAIN/MAJORCA, GREECE and ITALY are the most popular holiday destinations for the British. Nearly two-thirds of all holiday trips abroad are to these countries. The DHSS recommends TYPHOID vaccination for some areas in these countries – usually the hotter regions and where sanitation is primitive. As a general rule you should make sure your TETANUS vaccination is up-to-date and although POLIO is not now recommended by DHSS for European countries it might still be wise to have it.

Further Afield

If you are going to AFRICA, CENTRAL or SOUTH AMERICA, ASIA and parts of the FAR EAST, or even just passing through, you will need protection against other diseases.

MALARIA and YELLOW FEVER are caused by bites from certain types of mosquitoes. TYPHOID, CHOLERA and INFECTIOUS HEPATITIS are caused by poor sanitation.

Your Doctor Can Do Most Vaccinations

Check your requirements AT LEAST SIX WEEKS (preferably 2-3 months) before departure, with the DHSS, or with any vaccination centre. Check again just before you go in case regulations have changed. Your doctor should be able to give you all the necessary vaccinations, except YELLOW FEVER which is obtainable only at special vaccination centres. These are listed on page 12 of DHSS leaflet SA35 "Protect Your Health Abroad – this leaflet tells you how", which is free from all DHSS offices. British Airways Immunisation Centre (01 439 9584/5) and Thomas Cook's Vaccination Centre (01 499 4000) in Central London can do all vaccinations, including Yellow Fever. Remember to be vaccinated for places you are just passing through or making a stopover, if any of the above diseases is present.

If you are travelling to places where sanitation is primitive, you should consider protection against INFECTIOUS HEPATITIS. If in doubt, ask your doctor. If you are travelling in areas where medical facilities are not readily available, the DHSS advise you to be actively immunised against TETANUS if you have not been previously so immunised.

Useful Addresses

For up-to-date information about vaccination requirements, contact one of the following UK Government Health Departments:

ENGLAND	DHSS, Alexander Fleming House, London SE1 6BY. Tel. 01-407 5522 Ext. 6749
SCOTLAND	Scottish Home and Health Dept., St. Andrew's House, Edinburgh, EH1 3DE. Tel. 031-556 8501 Ext. 2438
WALES	Welsh Office, Cathays Park, Cardiff CF1 3NQ. Tel. Cardiff 825111 Ext. 3395
N. IRELAND	DHSS, Upper Newtownards Road, Belfast BT4 3SF. Tel. Belfast 63939 Ext. 2593

The list opposite is correct (at January 1984) for journeys DIRECT FROM BRITAIN, BUT CHECK, because regulations may change. If you are not travelling direct from Britain your requirements might be different especially in respect of CHOLERA and YELLOW FEVER.

RANK	COUNTRY	CHOLERA	ANTI-MALARIA TABLETS	TYPHOID	POLIO	YELLOW FEVER
1	France			R*		
2	Spain/Majorca/Canaries			R		
3	Greece			R		
4	Italy			R		
5	Belgium/Luxembourg					
6	USA					
7	Ireland (Republic of)					
8	Portugal/Azores/Madeira			R		
9	Gibraltar/Malta/Cyprus			R	·R+	
10	Netherlands					
11	West Germany					
12	Austria					
13	Switzerland					
14	Yugoslavia			R		
15	North Africa	R	R	R	R	
16	Canada					
17	Commonwealth Caribbean			R	R	
18	Denmark					
19	Middle East	R	R	R	R	
20	Eastern Europe					
	PLACE:					
	DATE VACCINATED					

SOURGE: DTI International Passenger Survey 1982: Holiday Visits

* Mediterranean coastal areas only.
R means that vaccination or preventative tablets are recommended by the DHSS for protection against disease.
R+ Azores and Madeira only.

21

VACCINATIONS AND PRECAUTIONS
FOR FARAWAY PLACES

RISK AREAS	DISEASE	HOW CAUGHT
Africa, Panama and South America	**YELLOW FEVER**	Bite from an infected AEDES mosquito
NONE	**SMALLPOX**	
Asia, Africa, Middle & Far East	**CHOLERA**	Contaminated water or to a lesser extent food.
Everywhere except Australia, New Zealand, Europe and North America	**POLIO**	Direct contact with an infected person, rarely by contaminated food or water.
Everywhere except NW Europe, NE USA, New Zealand and Australia	**TYPHOID**	Contaminated food or water
Everywhere but especially the Tropics	**TETANUS (LOCKJAW)**	Toxin producing bacteria enter the body through broken skin.
Countries where sanitation is primitive	**INFECTIOUS HEPATITIS (VIRAL HEPATITIS TYPE A)**	Contaminated food or water or contact with an infected person.
Africa, Central and South America, Asia, parts of the Middle East	**MALARIA**	Bite from an infected ANOPHELES mosquito.

For further details see DHSS leaflet SA35
"Protect your health abroad. This leaflet tells you how."

VACCINATION METHOD AND VALIDITY	YOU ARE PROTECTED FOR
1 inj. at least 10 days before leaving. Preferably 3 weeks apart from another live vaccine such as polio.	**10 YEARS.** 10 days after vaccination.
In 1980 the World Health Organisation declared that smallpox had been eradicated worldwide. No countries now require a certificate.	
2 injs. at least 10 days apart (usually 4-6 weeks). Not 100% effective.	**6 MONTHS.** 6 days after vaccination.
3 oral doses, with an interval of 6-8 weeks between the first and second doses and of 4-6 weeks between the second and third. Preferably not at the same time as Yellow Fever.	**10 YEARS.**
2 injs. 4-6 weeks apart. In urgent cases, the interval can be reduced to 10 days, giving protection for 1 year only.	**3 YEARS.** Or 1 year.
For people who have never been vaccinated, 2 injs. 6-12 weeks apart followed by a third 6-12 months later. If you have been previously vaccinated check with your doctor to see if you need a booster.	**5 TO 10 YEARS.**
No vaccine available, but can inject antiserum (gammaglobulin) to the disease which gives some protection. Check advisability with your doctor.	**3-6 MONTHS.**
ALWAYS OBTAIN ADVICE on the right tablets to take for the area to be visited from an immunisation centre or your doctor. **You must take the tablets before, during and for 4-6 weeks after your visit** even if you are only passing through an affected area or making a stop-over.	**THE PERIOD DURING WHICH YOU TAKE THE TABLETS.**

INSURANCE
SPEND A LITTLE AND SAVE A PACKET!

Travel anywhere, at home or abroad, carries certain risks. Even the best laid plans can sometimes go wrong. A major worry is the cost of medical treatment abroad and personal accident. All these risks can be covered by a "Holiday Insurance Package Policy" or by a "Selective Holiday Policy".

A STANDARD OR PACKAGE POLICY costs up to £14 per adult for a fortnight's cover in Europe and the Mediterranean area. Well worth it for the peace of mind. Premiums are usually higher for destinations further afield.

Check Your Policy.

Note the SCOPE of the POLICY, the EXCLUSIONS (the things the insurer won't pay for), the EXCESSES, and the RULES for MAKING A CLAIM, carefully.

A typical 'Package Policy' will cover you for the following:

1. **Medical & Emergency Expenses:**
   Usual Cover ... up to £100,000, and even unlimited with some policies

   In addition to the costs of medical aid, check that REPATRIATION is covered. You may need to be brought home after an accident or because of a sudden illness needing specialist treatment. Most insurers now include a 24-hour emergency service operated by companies such as Europ Assistance, Medex, or Transcare International. These specialists have multi-lingual co-ordinators who are expert at arranging on-the-spot assistance, payment of bills covered under the insurance and organising air ambulances for immediate repatriation in severe cases. You should make a note of UK telephone numbers in case you require to contact them for medical advice or assistance with repatriation.

   Additional HOTEL and TRAVEL EXPENSES related to sickness or injury and expenses incurred in returning home due to injury, illness, or death of a friend, relative, or business associate travelling with you are also normally covered.

   Medical expenses covered under a "Package Policy" may not be sufficient for **North America.** Consult your insurance broker or travel agent about any necessary additional cover.

With some policies you must disclose full details of any illness or medical condition from which you suffer, before the cover is issued, EVEN THOUGH THIS INFORMATION MAY NOT BE SPECIFICALLY REQUESTED. This sometimes includes PREGNANCY.

Exclusions: Of course, if you injure yourself by doing something irresponsible especially under the influence of alcohol, don't be surprised if the insurance company refuses to pick up the tab! A typical exclusion clause would read as follows: "Claims arising from suicide, insanity, intoxication, drugs other than prescribed by a qualified medical practitioner, mountaineering, winter sports (unless the appropriate premium has been paid), racing, speed or endurance tests, hazardous pursuits (e.g. pot holing, hang-gliding, underwater activities), air travel (other than as a fare paying passenger on a regular scheduled airline or licensed charter aircraft). Medical expenses recovered under a NHS reciprocal agreement abroad. Pregnancy which commenced prior to the holiday booking. Unreasonable care and attention."

Provident Associations

If you are a subscriber to one of the major Provident Association schemes such as PPP, BUPA, WPA, etc., then you will be covered on the same scales as your domestic cover. This will generally include specialist fees and hospital bills, although it will exclude General Practitioners, ambulances, out patient drugs and repatriation costs. Check with your own Provident Association for full details.

2. **Cancellation or Curtailment**
   Usual cover ... £75 to £1,000

If you have to CANCEL for reasons beyond your control, e.g. because of accident, illness, quarantine, jury service or witness summons, pregnancy (unknown when policy taken out), redundancy, you may be able to claim.

CURTAILMENT means you have to abandon your holiday and return to the UK for a number of reasons, e.g. illness of yourself or travelling companion, fire, theft, or flood at your private residence. In this event you may be able to claim a proportion of the cost of the holiday.

Exclusions: Disinclination to travel or financial circumstances other than redundancy. Failure of tour operator, airline etc.

3. **Personal Accident**
   Usual Cover ... £5,000 - £25,000

   If during the period of insurance you should die in an accident, or lose a limb(s) or one or both eyes or suffer permanent total disablement, you will be entitled to certain benefits.

   Exclusions: The exclusions are the same as for medical and emergency expenses.

4. **Baggage & Personal Effects**
   Usual Cover ... £500 - £1,500

   Luggage or articles of clothing which are lost or damaged on holiday are generally covered, with a single article limit of about £200. The RULES for MAKING A CLAIM are important:

   LOSSES MUST BE REPORTED TO THE LOCAL POLICE WITHIN 24 HOURS and a REPORT OBTAINED. Proof of notification will be needed when making a claim. The tour operator's representative or the carrier should also be told.

   Exclusions: Confiscation, detention or delay by customs or other officials. Normal wear and tear. Damage to fragile or brittle articles. Loss not properly reported, as above.

5. **Money, Tickets, Credit Cards**
   Usual Cover ... £200 - £250

   The cover and exclusions are approximately

the same as under baggage and personal effects.

6. **Personal Liability to Others**
   Usual Cover ... £250,000-£500,000
   This covers your legal liability to pay
compensation for accidental injury to or death of
Third Parties or accidental loss or damage of the
property of Third Parties.

   Exclusions: Claims arising from or connected
with racing, malicious acts, vehicles, aircraft,
motorboats or yachts.

   Certain policies cover you only for awards
made in UK courts.

7. **Delay ... Usually limited to £50 per person**
   Some policies pay compensation if your
departure is delayed beyond a specified period,
for example 12 hours, as a result of strike, industrial
action, adverse weather or breakdown of the
aircraft or sea vessel.

   A SELECTIVE POLICY enables you to obtain
insurance for longer periods than under a
'Package Policy' and to buy increased sums
insured for some risks and ignore others. For
example, if you are booking the day before you
leave, you might not need cancellation or
curtailment cover but you might want extended
medical cover.

RECIPROCAL HEALTHCARE AGREEMENTS

UK nationals, normally living in the UK, are
entitled to free or reduced cost medical treatment
when visiting another European country, New
Zealand or Hong Kong. Unlike the NHS in the UK
however, most of these countries do not offer a
comprehensive health service. Details of what you
are entitled to and how you go about getting it are

given in leaflets **SA 30** "Medical Costs Abroad –
what you need to know before you go" and **SA 36**
"How to get medical treatment in other European
Countries", available from DHSS offices.

In the EEC you need form **E111** as proof of
entitlement. An application form (CM1) for this is at
the back of leaflet SA 30. You should send this to
the DHSS 1 to 6 months before you go. In other
countries you may only need your UK passport
and/or NHS medical card.

There may be some charges for treatment,
hospital accommodation and ambulance transport.
The costs of repatriation are **never** covered. For
example:

Country	Documents	What is normally *free*	What *you pay* some charges for	Other information
AUSTRIA	UK passport	In-patient treatment in public wards of public hospitals.	10% of in-patient treatment of dependants. Prescribed medicines. All other medical services including treatment at a hospital out-patient department or doctor's surgery. Private treatment or accommodation in a public hospital.	
BELGIUM	E111	Nothing	Hospital treatment. Prescribed medicines. Other medical and dental treatment.	About 75% of charges are refunded by Belgian Sickness Insurance Fund. Fund. See SA36.
FRANCE	E111	Nothing	Hospital treatment. Dental treatment. Other medical care. Prescribed medicines.	70-80% of charges are refunded by French Sickness Insurance Office. See SA 36

Country	Documents	What is normally **free**	What **you pay** some charges for	Other information
GIBRALTAR	UK passport (Elll needed only if **not** UK national or national of Gibraltar	Hospital treatment in public wards of St. Bernards Hospital. Treatment at Casemates Health Centre.	Medical treatment elsewhere. Prescribed medicines (small charge). Dental treatment. But on weekdays in normal hours extractions are obtainable at St. Bernards Hospital for a nominal charge.	
GREECE	Elll	Nothing	Hospital treatment. Other medical treatment. Prescribed medicines. (There are often long waits for treatment in the public health service and conditions can be crowded).	Although costs can be refunded by the Greek Social Insurance Foundation, travel insurance cover for private medical treatment is STRONGLY recommended. See SA36.
IRISH REPUBLIC	No documents needed.	All medical and dental treatment. (Local Health Board will arrange for a consultation with a public health service doctor or dentist). Most hospital treatment arranged by a doctor in public ward of health service hospital. Prescribed medicines.	Nothing.	Make it clear to the hospital, doctor, or dentist that you wish to be treated under the European Community's Social Security regulations. You may be asked to complete a simple statement.
ITALY	Elll	Hospital treatment. Dental treatment. Other medical treatment.	Prescribed medicines.	See SA36.
LUXEMBOURG	Elll	Hospital treatment.	Dental treatment. Other medical treatment. Prescribed medicines.	Partial refund of charges by Luxembourg Sickness Insurance Office. See SA36.

Country	Documents	What is normally **free**	What **you pay** some charges for	Other information
MALTA (if staying less than 30 days)	UK passport or tourist permit.	Emergency treatment in Government hospital.	Non-Government hospital treatment. Treatment at doctor's surgery. Prescribed medicines.	
NETHER-LANDS (Holland)	E111	Hospital treatment. Other medical treatment.	Dental treatment. Prescribed medicines.	See SA36.
PORTUGAL	UK passport	In-patient treatment in the general ward of an official hospital.	Medical consultation at an official hospital or health clinic of the Medical Social Services. Private treatment and private accommodation in an official hospital. Auxilliary diagnostic facilities. Prescribed medicines.	If you are a Portuguese national resident in the UK, you will need to show a Portuguese passport and a certificate of UK Social Security Insurance
SPAIN SWITZERLAND USA AUSTRALIA	. . . do **not** have a reciprocal agreement with the UK so you will need comprehensive medical insurance.			
WEST GERMANY	E111	Hospital treatment. Dental treatment. Other medical treatment.	Prescribed medicines.	See SA36.

Source D.H.S.S.

The agreement only covers treatment by certain doctors and hospitals belonging to the local "public" health service. Private treatment is strongly recommended, especially in Greece, and for that you will need private insurance. ˙

So, wherever you are going, make sure you have comprehensive travel insurance to cover medical costs – don't rely entirely on the reciprocal healthcare agreements. But if you don't have any insurance, the E111 is essential.

TAKING YOUR CAR ABROAD

Green Card

All UK motor policies extend automatically to
meet the **minimum legal requirements** for third

party insurance in all EEC countries plus Austria, Czechoslovakia, German Democratic Republic, Finland, Hungary, Norway, Sweden and Switzerland. However, if you have an accident resulting in injury or damage beyond these requirements you could find yourself faced with heavy bills. The automatic extension of cover was introduced to enable frontier checks of insurance documents to be abolished, but to ensure that you have the same level of cover as you have in the UK you must obtain a **Green Card** from your insurance company.

Production of a Green Card is required at present at the frontiers of Bulgaria, Greece (despite their membership of the EEC), Iceland, Iran, Israel, Morocco, Poland, Rumania, Spain, Tunisia, Turkey and Yugoslavia. If you don't have one, you will be obliged to take out insurance at expensive short term rates before entry is permitted.

Spain

The Spanish authorities can detain you and/or your car following an accident unless a deposit is made against the possibility of your being found liable. Your insurer can supply you with a **Bail Bond** which acts as surety in these circumstances.

Caravans

You will probably need extra cover if you wish to take a trailer caravan abroad and an extra premium will normally secure this. Ensure that the caravan is noted on your Green Card.

If You Have An Accident

Report it to the local Motor Insurance Bureau, whose address is on the Green Card, and notify your insurance company in the UK or their local agent as soon as possible.

TRAVELLING – PAIN OR PLEASURE?

Travelling can be a chore, but there are several things you can do to make your journey more comfortable and enjoyable.

Pre-travel Rest and Food

At least two good nights sleep to alleviate the effects of nervous tension and travel fatigue, factors which can also contribute to travel sickness. A light meal before a journey helps to "settle" the stomach.

Airtravel

The air inside the cabin is slightly "thinner", that is, it contains less oxygen, than at sea level – equivalent to an altitude of about 2000 metres. This has no harmful effect on the body but enclosed gases in the body will increase in volume by as much as a third, especially in the intestines. The air is also comparatively dry, about 20% Relative Humidity, because of the air conditioning. This has a dehydrating effect.

Drink

Because of the dry atmosphere, you will lose more body water than usual through your lungs. So, to avoid this dehydrating effect, which is only noticeable after about 4 hours flying, it is wise to drink plenty of non-alcoholic fluids before and during the flight. Alcohol only makes matters worse because it speeds up dehydration. Fizzy drinks should be avoided because the bubbles will expand and make you feel bloated.

Clothing

Wear loose-fitting clothes because of the slight gas expansion and loose fitting shoes, because if you are sitting in one place for too long, blood tends to pool in your legs. This results in a slight swelling of your feet and ankles – that's why sometimes you can't get your shoes back on! Occasional walks along the aisle help to relieve this.

Bear in mind your destination. While wool is best for cold climates, cotton is perfect for warm countries, because it "breathes", that is it absorbs perspiration and allows it to evaporate, keeping you cool and comfortable in the process. Man-made fibres such as terylene or nylon are uncomfortable to wear in hot humid climates. Light colours reflect heat and therefore help to keep you cool. Hats and scarves protect your head and hair from the sun during the day. You will also need something to cover up and protect you from insect bites at night.

Good quality sunglasses protect your eyes from the glare of the sun, which can be made worse by reflection from light coloured buildings and water.

Smoking

With the thinner air, the carbon monoxide level in smokers blood is comparatively higher than normal. This effect is very slight, but enough to cause a headache and make you feel tired. The higher carbon monoxide and lower oxygen concentration in the blood could of course be significant to smokers who have heart problems.

"Popping"Ears

During climb or descent you may feel discomfort in your ears or experience some deafness as a result of the pressurisation changes mentioned above. Relieve this by yawning, swallowing hard, or pinching nose while breathing out.

Pregnancy

Women are not usually allowed on long flights if they are more than 35 weeks pregnant because of the possibility of the onset of labour. Always check with your doctor before a holiday abroad or a flight. In addition, certain vaccinations and drugs, including some of the malaria prophylactics and several anti-bacterials may not be suitable.

Special Arrangements for the Disabled

"Planning and Booking a Holiday: Information for the Disabled Holidaymaker", is the title of an information sheet produced by the Royal Association for Disability and Rehabilitation (RADAR, 25 Mortimer St., London W1N 8AB, tel. 01-637 5400) – a must for the disabled.

This very useful "checklist" tells you how to organise a holiday in conjunction with your travel agent/tour operator, and lists publications worth consulting.

British Rail, all airlines, and the airports authorities have special services for disabled passengers. All they need is advance warning of your particular requirements.

Jet Lag

The body has a natural daily cycle or rhythm which needs to be realigned when you travel by air in an east-west direction. For example, if you fly out of Heathrow at 6pm., arriving in Toronto 7½ hours later, your body thinks it's time for bed (1.30 am), but because you have crossed 5 time zones (5 hours time difference), it's only 8.30 pm in Toronto and time for dinner!

Obviously your body needs time to adjust to this, longer as you get older. Alcohol, stress and fatigue also make adjustment more difficult. Sleeping on the 'plane helps. Take it easy for the first couple of days. Full adjustment might take weeks.

You won't get much "jet lag" if you cross only one or two time zones, e.g. for trips to Greece, or Italy. You have to cross 5 time zones for the effects to be appreciable. It is most noticeable when flying west to east.

Altitude

As well as having to "acclimatise" to different climate, culture, and time-zone differences, you might also have to get used to the effects of altitude.

The higher you go, the thinner the air. In Mexico City (7,200 ft) for example, the air contains about the same amount of oxygen as the aircraft cabin mentioned above. This can make some people dizzy and short of breath until they adjust. Hardly noticeable if you are healthy and fit, but it could be a problem if you have a respiratory or cardio-vascular complaint. Ask your doctor if in doubt.

THE 4 'S' ENTIALS
SUN, SEA, SAND & SNOW

A "healthy", "golden" tan makes you look and feel good and gives you a big psychological boost – especially when you return home! The funny thing is that this tan is your body's automatic attempt to protect you from the sun's TANNING rays!

Sunlight – UV and IR rays

Light from the sun includes the infra-red (IR), visible, and ultraviolet (UV) wavebands. Infra-red radiation we feel as heat; our eyes respond to "visible" light; and ultraviolet is the component responsible for tanning.

There are three ULTRAVIOLET 'COLOURS': UVc, which is largely absorbed in the upper atmosphere; UVa and UVb, which get through. The short wavelength UVb rays BURN untanned or unprotected skin and are responsible for the longer term "deep" tan which develops after a few days sunbathing. The longer wavelength UVa rays which are milder but more deeply penetrating than UVb, are responsible for the initial tan.

Tanning

Ultraviolet light stimulates melanocytes, which are cells just below the surface of the skin, to produce MELANIN. The main role of this dark pigment is to protect us by absorbing or scattering any further UV light that falls on the skin and stop it penetrating the deeper layers. The more sun – the more melanin – the darker the skin (within limits) – that is the tanning process.

The degree to which you are able to tan depends on the amount of melanin your body can produce – this varies from person to person and race to race.

Sunscreens and SPFs

Since UV light tends to be harmful, burning you if you're not careful, SUNSCREENS are an essential part of any holiday package. Properly formulated sunscreens protect your skin until your body has produced enough-melanin to defend itself and has adapted to its sudden exposure to sunlight.

Pick a **wide-spectrum water resistant** suncream which filters out both UVa and UVb rays.

Choose the **Sun Protection Factors (SPFs)** most suitable for your personal skin and the place you are visiting. SPFs are a guide to the degree of protection given by a sunscreen. Factor 5 for example, means that you can stay in the sun five times longer than you can without protection. Use two or three SPFs, starting with a high number for the first few days, working down as your tan develops.

Sunbathe with care at first

For the first few days you should not sunbathe in Northern Europe between 11am and 3pm or in places nearer the equator between 10am and 4pm. Gradually build up exposure from 15 minutes for unprotected skin on the first day.

The closer you are to the equator, and the higher the altitude, the greater is the need for higher SPFs than if you were sunbathing in the UK.

The skin on your face is especially sensitive. You should limit exposure and use a high SPF or even a total sunblock. Wear a hat.

Sea, sand, snow, and white buildings reflect the sun's rays. This increases the amount of UV actually falling on the skin and can speed-up burning. Wet skin is more easily penetrated by UV, so enhancing the burning effect. UV also gets through heavy cloud cover, catching out the unwary.

Overdoing it! – Sunburn

Because of our indoor lifestyle, most of us suffer sunburn to a greater or lesser extent no matter how careful we are.

SUNBURN can be soothed with a CALAMINE containing LOTION. If you develop a temperature and feel ill, cool yourself with cold water sponging or take a cold bath in a well ventilated area. Relax and rest. Take plenty of non-alcoholic fluids. If you are badly burnt, or if you have a temperature, seek medical attention right away.

Excessive Sensitivity

If you burn more quickly than usual, ask yourself – is it a drug I am taking or a skin application I am using?

Many medicines as well as the contraceptive pill can make your skin extremely sensitive to sunlight. Some cosmetics, perfumes, colognes, even deodorant soaps can cause skin irritation and rashes in strong sunlight.

Other UV hazards

Excessive exposure to UV (mainly UVb) leads to permanent change or premature ageing of the skin. In effect, the more sunbathing you do, the quicker your skin will "wear out", become wrinkled and leathery and lose its elasticity. Too much sun also weakens the body's natural defences and can lead to certain skin diseases including cancer.

So, sunbathe wisely and return home with the best souvenir of all – a beautiful tan!

EXTREME OF TEMPERATURE – HEAT EXHAUSTION & HEAT STROKE

Excessive heat can lead to more serious problems than the "normal" sunburn we all suffer. These extreme conditions, although comparatively rare, merit a brief mention because you may hear the terms from time-to-time. In all cases, **consult a doctor as soon as possible.**

Heat Exhaustion is a condition caused by loss of salt and water from the body as a result of heavy sweating and inadequate or inappropriate fluid replacement. This normally affects people

41

performing unaccustomed hard physical work or exercise during acclimatisation in very hot and humid climates.

Common symptoms are exhaustion, restlessness, nausea, dizziness, headache, cold and clammy skin, and in more severe cases sickness and muscle cramps.

Relax and rest in a cool place and replace lost fluids and salts, by sipping water, or a solution made up of half a level teaspoonful of salt in half a litre (1 pint) of water.

If you don't feel better fairly soon, see a doctor.

Heat Stroke can come on suddenly, as the name suggests, or be preceded by heat exhaustion. It is a very serious condition caused by very high environmental temperature or by a feverish illness, leading to a sudden rise in body temperature. This develops when the body's "thermostatic" sweating mechanism fails.

It is most important to get the body's temperature back to normal as quickly as possible by immersing in a cool bath or wrapping in a wet cold sheet. After that, rest, lying down, wrapped in a dry sheet in a cool room and drink plenty of fluids.

TRAVELLER'S DIARRHOEA
MONTEZUMA'S REVENGE!

Diarrhoea can be a real killjoy on a trip abroad. It can be caused by all sorts of things ranging from greasy food to cholera, but "Traveller's Diarrhoea" ALMOST ALWAYS results from infection with bacteria, usually E. Coli picked up from contaminated water or food.

Food for Thought

The key to avoiding infection, which might result in diarrhoea, is simply to take care over food, drink and hygiene and ensure that your vaccinations are up-to-date. With a bit of commonsense and caution you should have nothing to worry about.

Water may be contaminated through inadequate sewage disposal and chlorination facilities even in main towns and cities in "underdeveloped" countries. Unless the water is known to be safe, "sterilise" it by boiling for ten minutes or by chlorination with water purification tablets. Once sterilised, store in a sealed or covered container, preferably in a 'fridge. Don't even brush your teeth in water you are not sure about.

Otherwise drink only a known brand of bottled water (Evian, Perrier etc) and soft drinks, bought from reputable sources – not street vendors!

If the water is contaminated, there is a chance that MILK, CREAM, BUTTER, YOGHURT, ICE-CREAM, SOFT DRINKS and ICE will also be contaminated.

MEAT and FISH should be fresh, well cooked and served hot – but not reheated. Be wary of COLD MEATS, COLD BUFFETS, SALADS and UNCOOKED VEGETABLES. THIN-SKINNED FRUITS must be undamaged. Peel all fruit, including tomatoes. SEAFOOD are a notorious hazard, if they come from polluted waters, especially SHELLFISH which can concentrate micro-organisms in their bodies.

Avoid places with poor sanitation and standards of hygiene, especially restaurants – if the floors and tables are dirty, what will the kitchen be like?

Fluid Losses and Dehydration

Diarrhoea can be inconvenient, uncomfortable, and sometimes even painful. It isn't dangerous in itself, but the dehydration that can occur as a result of the salt and water lost from the body during attacks of diarrhoea can be dangerous.

Babies, infants, the infirm and the elderly are particularly at risk here. Always see a doctor right away if a baby gets diarrhoea.

The lost fluids and salts can be replaced by mouth. Ideally you should take a properly formulated GLUCOSE/ELECTROLYTE SOLUTION, but in the absence of such a product a simple first-aid solution can be made as follows:

Dissolve ONE **LEVEL** 5ML SPOONFUL OF SALT (3.5g) and EIGHT LEVEL SPOONFULS OF SUGAR (40g) **OR** FOUR OF GLUCOSE (20g) in **AT LEAST** ONE LITRE (1¾ pints) of DRINKING WATER.

It is very important not to exceed the salt and sugar quantities and to use a litre of water, **or more** if you are not sure.

As a general guide, an adult may need to drink 400 mls (nearly ¾ of a pint) and a child 200 mls of this solution after each visit to the toilet. Drink "little and often", otherwise the salt might make you feel sick.

In addition to helping put back the water and salts, the glucose also provides some "instant" energy while you are off foods.

Fluid Balance

You will also need PLENTY of other fluids such as water, weak tea, or some bland drink such as very dilute barley water, to keep you fit, especially in hot climates.

As a rule-of-thumb, you should drink about **one pint of fluid for every ten degrees fahrenheit in twenty four hours –** more if you are exercising – but not strong alcoholic beverages.

A simple way to check that your fluid intake is sufficient is to observe your urine. It should be almost clear. If it is yellow or dark in colour, then you are dehydrating and you should increase your fluid intake.

Medicines for Diarrhoea

Diarrhoea quite often clears up by itself, but if it persists for more than a few hours you may wish to take an anti-diarrhoeal medicine to help reduce its severity and relieve symptoms. Products such as MIXTURE OF KAOLIN AND MORPHINE have

45

been found useful over the years. They usually contain an adsorbant together with a small amount of drug to reduce mobility of the gut. Ask your pharmacist to recommend the most suitable medicine for you.

ANTIBIOTIC and SULPHONAMIDE preparations should never be used except under medical supervision.

If an attack of diarrhoea persists for more than 48 hours you should consult a doctor, because it may not be simply "Traveller's Diarrhoea" and may require treatment with prescription drugs under medical supervision.

If you get severe watery diarrhoea in a CHOLERA epidemic area, see a doctor right away. Take plenty of fluids but DON'T take any medicines for your diarrhoea until your doctor says so.

Side Effects

Medicines you are taking may not be completely absorbed. For example, if a woman taking the BIRTH CONTROL PILL gets diarrhoea for more than one day, she may not be protected for that cycle.

So, STOP ALL SOLID FOODS AND MILK PRODUCTS, until your appetite returns and DRINK PLENTY of non-alcoholic fluids. If it persists for more than a few hours, take a mild ANTIDIARRHOEAL medicine; and make sure that Montezuma doesn't ruin your trip!

TYPHOID IN PERSPECTIVE
THERE'S NOT A LOT ABOUT!

Typhoid is a disease caused by bacteria belonging to the salmonella family. It can be caught anywhere in the world – even the United Kingdom. However, it is predominantly found in countries or areas with poor hygiene and inadequate sewage disposal arrangements, which result in contamination of drinking water and food.

You can catch typhoid only by swallowing the typhoid organism. If you don't swallow the organism, you won't get the disease. It is not transmitted from body to body by personal contact nor is it transmitted through the air.

In countries with unsafe water supply, this is the commonest means of transmitting typhoid. Food may also be contaminated, and milk is probably second to water as the vehicle of infection in countries where hygiene is poor and pasteurisation is not carried out routinely.

The organism will only live in man. Some people who become infected become carriers, that is to say they continue to excrete the organism for a long time while showing no signs of having a recognisable illness. These carriers may pass the organisms from their guts into the sewage or they may directly infect food by touching it with unwashed hands. However, even if your food is handled by a carrier, it does not follow that you will automatically get typhoid. For some reason most carriers only very rarely transmit the disease.

To put the incidence of typhoid into perspective, national statistics show that on average about 200 cases of typhoid occur annually in England and Wales. These result in one or two deaths. Of the reported cases, ten to fifteen per cent are due to typhoid infection caught in this country; the rest are due to infection caught abroad. For example, in 1982, 21 cases were contracted in Britain, 16 in Mediterranean countries and 93 in the Indian Sub-continent.

Bearing in mind the millions of people who travel abroad each year, the risk to the average British holidaymaker is therefore very small.

There is no reason for undue anxiety over this relatively rare, though admittedly serious, disease. It is not the killer that it was in the 19th century and nowadays it can usually be treated effectively with modern antibiotics.

The risk of catching it can be reduced even further by typhoid immunisation before you go to a country where the disease is fairly common, which includes all Mediterranean countries, and by following the simple commonsense precautions about food, water and hygiene outlined previously.

SOME SIMPLE REMEDIES
FOR COMMON AILMENTS

Travel Sickness

If you suffer from this you should ask your pharmacist or doctor to select the most suitable preparation for you. The following may also be helpful: Choose the most stable part of the vehicle. Don't sit in the tail of an aircraft, or over the wheels in a bus, or on the back seat of a car. In a ship, try to keep amidships and lie down if posssible. Try to keep the head as immobile as possible and get plenty of fresh air. Keep away from kitchen and diesel smells. Avoid fried or fatty foods, alcohol to excess, and smoking, all of which may aggravate the stomach and make you sick. Don't get excited or anxious before the journey.

Antihistamines can prevent travel sickness if taken before your journey begins, but are no use once the symptoms are established. One word of warning though – all these preparations are sedative, which means they may cause drowsiness, impair driving performance and enhance the effects of alcohol and other drugs. If you are affected like this, don't drive!

Hangover

Since there is no cure for hangover, some of the following suggestions might help you recover.

First, never drink on an empty stomach. Second, don't mix your drinks. But if you must, beer followed by wine will cause you less problems than wine followed by beer. Third, since alcohol, like coffee, actually dehydrates you, drink water, and plenty of it, before you retire.

Drinks low in 'congeners' such as vodka and gin, cause less headaches than those high in congeners such as brandy and port.

Over-indulgence causes excess production of acid in the stomach which can be counteracted with any proprietary antacid. Mineral water, which is slightly alkaline, will also help.

Fresh orange juice the morning after seems to work wonders, possibly because of the Vitamin C and the potassium content.

Low blood sugar, which makes you feel weak, can be rectified with bread and jam, marmalade, or honey, or a dilute glucose drink such as orange squash.

Plenty of non-alcoholic drinks will replace the fluids lost and a couple of pain killers should clear the headache.

Finally, take a tip from the French – drink water, at least glass-for-glass with your wine – you'll enjoy it more, spend less, and avoid the headaches.

Toothache

If you lose a filling or break a tooth and you can't get to a dentist, then a few drops of OIL OF CLOVES on a cotton bud applied to the open inflamed tooth will bring temporary relief. This won't work if the pain is due to an abscess inside the tooth. Aspirin or paracetamol will also help to kill the pain. If you get sore or inflamed gums, some relief will be obtained by swishing around your mouth a solution made by dissolving a level teaspoonful of TABLE SALT in a beaker of WARM WATER.

Blisters

In general DON'T BURST BLISTERS because of the risk of infection of the area under the skin. However, in certain circumstances this may not be practicable, so, if you must: wash the blister with antiseptic solution; sterilise a needle by passing it through a flame or by immersing in boiling water; pierce the blister in two places near its base; absorb fluid that emerges on clean cotton wool or gauze; and cover with a dry dressing until healed.

Constipation

The most natural treatment for simple constipation is to increase the amount of dietary fibre in your diet. This is easily achieved by eating more bread, wheatbran breakfast cereals, potatoes, "pulses" including peas, beans and lentils, fruit and leafy vegetables (but don't overcook them!). Drink plenty of NON-ALCOHOLIC FLUIDS as well.

If this fails a gentle LAXATIVE might help but if the condition persists you should consult a doctor.

Indigestion

Antacids will ease an upset stomach. The discomfort is usually due to irritation of the stomach lining caused by over-indulgence in rich food and alcohol.

The choice of antacid is largely a matter of personal preference. Liquid preparations may be slightly more effective than solids but tablets are more portable.

Sore Throat

Relief from sore throats may be obtained by taking an antiseptic THROAT LOZENGE or by gargling with HALF A SPOONFUL OF TABLE SALT or TWO ASPIRINS dissolved in a beaker of WARM WATER.

Athlete's Foot

This infection is caused by a fungus – Tinea pedis – usually picked up around swimming pools and in shower rooms. The skin between the toes becomes white, sodden and cracked. The cleft between the 4th and 5th toes is almost always affected. Prevention is difficult but wearing shoes or "flip-flops" around the pool will help. Avoid nylon socks. Change socks at least daily, and take care to dry the skin between the toes. Antifungal creams and powders will stop the itching and clear up the problem – don't forget to dust your shoes as well.

Cold Sores (Herpes Simplex 1)

"Cold sores" are occasional eruptions on the face caused by a virus called Herpes Simplex 1 (not to be confused with Herpes Simplex 2 – the usual cause of genital herpes). After infection the virus can lie dormant in the body until certain conditions "activate" it, when it comes to the surface of the skin and causes the characteristic "cold sore" eruptions on the face. The mechanism isn't fully understood but it seems to be linked to skin inflammation such as mild sunburning and tends to occur when you are recovering from a cold or other illnesses. Applying a little cold cream to prevent cracking at the crusting stage is about all you can do.

Venereal Disease

The initial signs are often very slight and may be overlooked; thus the more dangerous and painful secondary forms of certain sexually transmitted diseases can develop without previous warning.

GONORRHOEA is just one of many diseases which may be transmitted by any type of sexual encounter. If you do suspect VD, don't delay – have a check-up at one of the special clinics that are found in most cities. Self-medication or treatment from unqualified practitioners is dangerous to you and may lull you into a false sense of security. Remember, some strains of bacteria are resistant to penicillin.

GENERAL FIRST-AID GUIDANCE
Text approved by
The British Red Cross Society

Some basic general knowledge of first-aid is useful at any time because you never know when accidents will happen to you, your family or associates, and there can be nothing worse than the feeling of despair if you can't help.

The object of first aid is to save life and prevent any deterioration in the state of a casualty until placed, if necessary, in the care of a doctor, or removed to hospital.

Proper training is essential if you are to tackle serious emergencies, but the following notes may help you to cope until skilled help arrives.

For details of **first-aid courses,** contact the British Red Cross Society, the St. Johns Ambulance Association, or the St Andrews Ambulance Association. Their telephone numbers are in the book.

Action at the Scene
If necessary, get someone to 'phone for an ambulance or doctor immediately. Look out for and avoid any danger to yourself and the casualty. Keep clear of gas, smoke, electric current, switch off car engines, warn approaching traffic, do not allow smoking.

PRIORITIES
1. Breathing

Firstly, check that all the casualties are breathing.

If the casualty's heart is beating but he is not breathing, **mouth-to-mouth resuscitation** must be started at once **before any other treatment is given.** Never try this if the casualty is still breathing. The 4 steps are:

(a) **Open the Airway.** An unconscious casualty's airway may be narrowed or blocked making breathing difficult or even impossible. To establish a clear airway: get the casualty on his back, then:

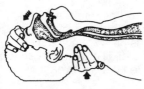 

Place one hand under the neck and the other on the forehead and tilt the head backwards. This will open the air passage.

Transfer your hand from the neck and push the chin upwards. The tilted jaw will lift the tongue forward, clear of the airway.

(b) **Clear the Airway.** Quickly tilt the head on its side and remove any obstruction with your fingers, e.g. false teeth.

(c) **Check breathing.** You can hear and feel if he is breathing by placing your ear above his mouth. Look along the chest and abdomen to see if there is any movement.

(d) **Mouth-to-Mouth Ventilation.** The technique is not difficult, but it is better to learn it by practise on a manikin at a first-aid class. Remember – **don't try this if the casualty is breathing.**

Mouth-to-Mouth Ventilation

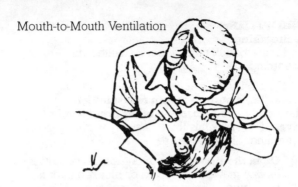

With the head tilted back and the chin forward, the airway and mouth are open. Pinch the casualty's nostrils with your free hand. Take a deep breath and sealing your lips round his mouth, blow into it steadily and smoothly. The casualty's chest should rise as his lungs fill. When you lift your mouth off, his chest will fall. Turn your head to one side to look for this while taking a breath of fresh air.

You should give the first three or four breaths quickly without waiting for complete lung deflation between breaths, to make sure that the lungs receive a great deal of air at the start. Thereafter, repeat inflations at your normal breathing rate. Keep this up until a skilled person takes over.

In the case of **children,** seal your lips round the mouth and nose and breath gently into the lungs, just enough to get the chest moving at a rate of about 20 breaths per minute.

If the casualty's chest fails to rise, the airway may not be fully open, so readjust the position of the head and jaw and try again. If there is still no ventilation, the airway may be blocked, and you will have to treat as for **choking** – see later.

Once normal breathing is restored, turn the

casualty into the **Recovery Position.** In this position the tongue will move away from the back of the throat and fluids will be able to drain safely out of the mouth.

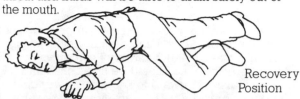

Recovery
Position

If the heart is not beating, external chest compression is needed.

This should not be attempted until you have learnt the skill at a class.

2. Bleeding

What follows here concerns major external bleeding which is obviously life-threatening. Minor cuts and grazes are dealt with later.

If the injury is to a limb, raise it, but don't do this if the limb is fractured.

Press firmly on the wound to flatten the cut blood vessels and thus stop or control bleeding. If a wound is gaping, press its edges together with thumb and/or fingers, or press a pad of clean material hard over the wound and then bandage it, firmly but not so tightly as to cut off circulation. If blood seeps through the dressing, don't remove it. Apply another dressing or pad and firmly bandage. Tourniquets should not be used by inexperienced people, because they cut off the blood supply and therefore the oxygen supply to the entire limb.

Loose dirt and debris can be wiped from the surface of a wound with a clean cloth, or rinsed with cold water. If something is embedded in the skin, don't attempt to remove it because it may be plugging the wound, and pulling it out may cause further injury. Leave removal to a doctor.

3. Unconsciousness

An unconscious casualty is likely to have his breathing obstructed if he is left on his back.

Follow the steps above: check airway, breathing, circulation, and take appropriate action, then control bleeding. If the casualty is breathing normally, place in the **Recovery Position** as illustrated. The head should be tilted back and the chin pushed forward to keep the airway open. The limbs prop the body on its side with the arm bent at right angle at the elbow, and the upper leg bent at right angle at the hip and knee. The lower arm should be stretched out along the back. This position is stable and reasonably safe.

Don't move a casualty with suspected broken bones, especially a spinal injury unless difficulty in breathing makes it essential. **Do not give anything** by mouth to an unconscious casualty.

4. Broken Bones

Deal with breathing, bleeding, and unconsciousness first. If you suspect a fracture, treat as a definite fracture. Do not move the casualty unless in danger because the jagged ends of broken bones can cause further internal damage if allowed to move – especially where the spine or neck are involved. Support the injured limb by hand to prevent movement and make the casualty as comfortable as possible. If the casualty must be moved, secure the injured part to a sound part of the body e.g. by supporting the arm in a sling which is strapped to the chest or by tying the legs together – firmly enough to support and prevent movement but not so tightly as to affect circulation.

IN ALL OF THE ABOVE CASES, THE CASUALTY MUST BE REFERRED TO A DOCTOR.

OTHER INJURIES
Burns and Scalds
Unless severe, immediately cool the area, preferably under a cold water tap, or by soaking in a harmless clean cool liquid (milk, soft drinks, beer, etc.) for at least 10 minutes. Remove anything constrictive such as rings, watches, in case of swelling. Cover with a loose dressing, or gently wrap in clean fabric.

Superficial, but extensive burns (greater than the area of the palm of the hand) should be seen by a doctor. Deeper burns, even though small (1" square or so) or those arising from electrical contact, must also be referred to a doctor.

N.B. **Do not** remove anything that is sticking to a burn.
Do not apply lotions, ointments, fats, butter or oil.
Do not burst blisters or otherwise handle the area.
Do not remove cooled, charred clothing – it will be sterile.

Chemical Contamination
Take care to protect yourself from the chemical. Contact with acid, other corrosive materials or toxic substances should be washed off thoroughly and treated as a burn above. Remove and dispose of contaminated clothing.

Choking
Most obstructions in the windpipe will be removed by coughing, but where this does not work, four hard slaps between the shoulder blades with the heel of the hand, should dislodge the object, with the casualty bent forward to take advantage of gravity.

Drowning
Quickly remove any obstructions and start artificial ventilation, in the water if possible, if the casualty is not breathing.
Don't wait until you get to dry land.

If you are within your own depth, use one arm to support the casualty's body and the other to support the head and seal the nose while you perform artificial ventilation.

In deeper waters, give the occasional breath while towing to the shore.

Don't worry about emptying water out of the lungs – even in someone who has drowned, there may be very little water actually in the lungs.

When breathing restarts, put the casualty into the Recovery Position, remove wet clothing, dry off, and keep warm by covering with spare clothes and towels.

Arrange for removal to hospital.

Electric Shock
a. Domestic Supply

Be careful not to touch the casualty until you have switched off the power supply at the mains, removed the plug, or wrenched the cable free. Don't handle a suspect appliance.

If you can't break the current for some reason, use a dry insulating object such as wood (a stick or chair) to lever free the casualty. Remember that dampness on the skin or on the floor can conduct electricity. Then check breathing and start resuscitation if necessary. Treat any burns as potentially serious.

b. High Voltage Supply

Contact with high voltage currents found in power lines and overhead railway cables is usually immediately fatal. Don't approach the casualty because the electricity may 'arc' and electrocute you. Stay at least 20 yards away. Inform the police.

Fainting

A faint is a brief loss of consciousness caused by a temporary reduction in the flow of blood to the brain. The aim of first-aid is to position the casualty so that gravity helps increase the flow of blood to the brain.

To relieve an oncoming faint, sit the casualty down and lower his head between his knees. If the casualty loses consciousness, treat as described under 'PRIORITIES' above.

Foreign Body in the Eye

Prevent casualty from rubbing the eye. Flush the open eye using clean water from a tap or jug, with the head tilted towards the affected side so that the water will drain out over the cheek, away from the 'good' eye. If this is unsuccessful, or no water is available, and provided it is not sticking to the eye, lift the foreign body off using the damp corner of a clean handkerchief. If the object is under the upper lid, pull the upper lid downwards and outwards over the lower lid. If the foreign body is not brushed off by the eyelashes, then ask the casualty to blink the eye under water in the hope that it will float off.

If the object is on the coloured part of the eye, or if it is embedded in, or sticking to the eyeball, do not attempt to remove it. Lightly cover the eye with a pad and send the casualty to a doctor.

If the foreign body is poisonous or corrosive, prolonged irrigation of the eye is necessary.

Gassing

Move the casualty to fresh air but, in the case of smoke from fires, make sure that whoever does this is wearing suitable respiratory protection. If breathing has stopped, start resuscitation and continue until breathing is restored or until medical, nursing, or ambulance personnel take over. If the casualty needs to go to hospital make sure a note of the gas involved is sent with him.

Heart Attack

All severe pains in the chest (or upper abdomen) should be regarded as potentially

61

serious and requiring the services of a doctor.

If the casualty is conscious, assist him into a **half-sitting position with head and shoulders supported and knees bent.)** This position eases the work of the heart. Loosen tight clothing. Ensure that he has a good supply of air and is kept cool. If the casualty becomes unconscious, but is breathing normally, place in the Recovery Position.

If the breathing and heartbeat stop, carry out the resuscitation procedure.

Minor Cuts and Grazes

Superficial wounds should be cleaned thoroughly with soap and water or with an antiseptic wipe, then covered with an appropriate dressing – either a sticking plaster or for larger areas preferably with a non-adherent absorbent material, such as gauze, and tape down the edges.

Nosebleed

Support the casualty in the sitting position with his head slightly forward. Loosen clothing around the neck. Tell him to pinch firmly the soft part of his nose for about 10 minutes.

Don't disturb the clot, or blow nose for several hours.

If the bleeding does not stop, or if it recurs, the casualty should receive medical attention.

Poisoning (including alcohol)

Check breathing and be prepared to resuscitate. If the casualty is breathing but unconscious, place in the Recovery Position. If conscious, but the lips and mouth appear to be stained by having taken a corrosive substance, then dilute the poison by getting the casualty to sip quantities of fluids, such as milk or water (unsalted). Otherwise do nothing except check on his condition. **Do not make the casualty vomit because this may endanger breathing.** Rush him

to hospital and send samples of the poison
with him.

Sprains and Strains

A cold compress can ease pain and reduce
swelling. Rest and support the injured part in the
most comfortable position for the casualty. Apply
a firm bandage over a thin layer of cotton wool
and elevate the limb. In cases of doubt, or where
pain and swelling persist, send to a doctor.

GENERAL

Hygiene, Treatment Position, Drinks

Wash your hands if possible before treating
a casualty.

Avoid breathing over, or touching the face of
dressings, or open injuries.

The casualty should be seated or lying down
while being treated.

Unconscious casualties should be placed in
the Recovery Position.

In general, nothing should be given by mouth
to a casualty, as he could have breathing
endangered by vomiting. In minor cases of shock,
faints and burns, and when the casualty has
swallowed a corrosive poison, sips of water may
be given but in all other cases, a thirsty patient
can only have his lips moistened with water.

BITES, STINGS AND CREEPY CRAWLY THINGS!

The chances of being bitten by a shark are practically nil but look out for the following:

Jellyfish

Keep well away from the Portuguese Man-O-War, the most dangerous jellyfish in European waters. It has a pale blue body and long tentacles with barbed stingers. If stung, rub the barbs off with wet sand, then apply cooling lotion or sprays and cold compresses as for wasps and bees.

Sea Urchins

If you stand on Sea Urchins their long black spines will break off after they have pierced your skin and are hard to remove. MAGNESIUM SULPHATE PASTE (available at pharmacies) applied to the skin, will draw the spines to the surface. Prevention is better than cure – wear something on your feet – especially near rocks.

Mosquitos (and Midges too)

These insects bite between dusk and dawn. Not all mosquitoes transmit disease of course, but their bites are still very irritating. You can protect yourself from being bitten by: 1. Keeping well covered up after dark (wear light coloured clothes as dark clothing attracts mosquitoes); 2. Not wearing perfumes, perfumed deodorants or after-shave lotion which attract insects; 3. Mosquito "proofing" your windows or bed; 4. Spraying your bedroom with an insecticide; 5. Using an insect repellant on your skin – diethyl toluamide is reckoned to be the best.

Malaria

Malaria is widespread in tropical and subtropical areas of the world, for example: India; Bangladesh; Sri Lanka; parts of China; Brazil; Thailand; and Africa South of the Sahara.

It is spread by the bite of a female anopheles mosquito that has been infected by the malaria parasite.

There is no vaccine. You must take anti-malaria tablets which work by eliminating the parasites from the body. This can take up to six weeks after you have left a malaria zone, which is why you **must** keep taking the tablets when you return.

Ask your vaccination centre which tablets are suitable for the area you are visiting or passing through. In particular, ask the doctor which tablets to take if you are pregnant or taking young children, because some tablets may be more suitable than others, and some are "prescriptions only."

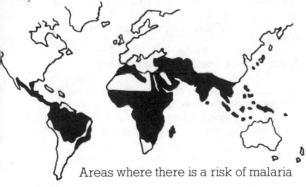

Areas where there is a risk of malaria

Note: Malaria is NOT a risk in: Hong Kong; Taiwan; Singapore; The West Indies except Haiti.

Dogs and Cats

RABIES is a viral infection of the central nervous system to which man and all warm-blooded animals are susceptible. It is a serious hazard occuring in all continents except Australasia and Antarctica. You can get it if you are bitten, scratched or EVEN LICKED by an infected dog, cat, fox or other animal. When symptoms develop it is nearly always fatal. So when abroad, avoid all animals as a general rule.

If bitten you should wash the wound immediately with copious amounts of soapy water or detergent, preferably under a running tap. If water is not available, use cold tea, beer, Coke, etc. Apply alcohol as well if you can. Take the owner's name, address, and telephone number and give him yours. Tell him to contact you if the animal gets sick or dies within 2 weeks. If wild or stray, note the animal's description, the place and the date. Go immediately to the nearest hospital for proper wound cleaning, your TETANUS "BOOSTER" if necessary and vaccination against rabies, if recommended by the doctor.

See your doctor as soon as you get back to Britain.

Stone-Fish, Sting-Ray, Weever Fish

The stone-fish lives in coral reefs and looks like a stone. The weever-fish lives below sand or shingle at the sea's edge.

They all have bony spines covered by venom-secreting tissues. These venoms cause intense local pain, but fortunately they are very "unstable" and can be rapidly deactivated by heat.

The treatment is to wash the wound immediately with cold salt water, then immerse the part stung in the hottest water bearable for a few seconds, then remove to prevent blistering. Repeat until pain no longer occurs (possibly 30 mins.).

Wasps and Bees

If the sting is left in the skin, scratch it out with a fingernail. DO NOT RUB OR SQUEEZE THE SKIN – this will just spread the venom. Antihistamine creams relieve pain and control swelling if applied immediately. The application of ICE and COLD COMPRESSES followed by CALAMINE LOTION will also be effective. For stings in the mouth, apply crushed ice to reduce swelling and seek medical help.

Snakes

Normally snakes only bite humans if they are frightened – as a defensive reaction after being disturbed. They often shelter under vegetation, among rocks, or behind fallen logs, so be careful where you walk. A walking stick is useful because the snake may strike at the stick rather than you.

If you are bitten by a snake don't try to kill it or you may be bitten again. Stay calm and don't rush about – activity increases your circulation and thus the speed of absorption of the toxin. Wipe the skin and cover with a clean cloth. NEVER cut the wound or squeeze it. Get medical attention as soon as possible.

Scorpions

The sting of most scorpions is like a severe wasp sting – so treat accordingly. But in some parts of the world, in particular South and Central America, scorpion stings can be more serious, particularly for the young, the elderly and the unwell.

DICTIONARY
Ummh! What's The Word For . . . ?

English	Francais
Accident	accident
Ambulance	ambulance
Ankle	cheville
Arm	bras
Aspirin	aspirine
Baby	bébé
Back	dos
Bandage	bandage

Since this book is about health, a few foreign words with the emphasis on pharmacy or medicine might help communications in the event of an accident or illness.

If you can speak the language, you know how to form the following words into sentences; if you can't, you might manage by just pointing the appropriate words out to the person you are dealing with.

Some words, like allergy, antihistamine, asthma, deodorant, diabetic, indigestion, insect, muscle, passport, pharmacy, police, vaccination, are almost the same in French, Spanish and Italian, so they are not included in the table.

This section is no substitute for a proper dictionary or phrase book, of course.

Espanol	Italiano
accidente	incidente
ambulansa	ambulanza
tobillo	caviglia
brazo	braccio
aspirina	aspirina
nino	bambino
espalda	schiena
venda	benda

English	Francais
Bee	abeille
Bite (as insect)	piqure
Blister	ampoule
Blood	sang
Bone	os
Burn	brûlure
Calamine cream (sunburn cream)	crème à brûlure du soleil
Car	voiture
Cold (temperature)	froid
A head cold	un rhume
Constipation	constipation
Contact lens	lenses à contat
Cotton wool	ouate
Cough	toux
A cut	coupure
Diarrhoea	diarrheé
Doctor	docteur
Dog	chien
Ear	oreille
Elbow	conde

Español	Italiano
abeja	ape
picadura	puntura
ampolla	vescica
sangre	sanque
hueso	osso
quemadura	bruciatura
crema para quemaduras	crema per bruciature da sole
coche	macchina
frio	freddo
resfriado	rafreddore
costipado	stitichezza
lentes de contacto	lenti a contatto
algodón	ovatta
tosa	tosse
cortadura	taglio
diarrea	diarrea
medico	dottore
perro	cane
oreja	orecchio
codo	gomito

English	Francais
Emergency	crise
Face	visage
Finger	doit
Fire	feu
Foot	pied
Hair	cheveux
Hand	maim
Hay fever	rhume des foins
Head	tête
Headache	mal de tête
Heart	coeur
Hospital	hôpital
Hot (temperature)	chaud
Insurance	assurance
Jellyfish	méduse
Knee	genoux
Moisturiser	moiteur
Money	argent
Mosquito	moustique
Mouth	bouche

Espanol	Italiano
emergenciá	emergenza
cara	viso
dedo	dito
fuego	fuoco
pie	piede
pelo	capelli
mano	mano
fiebre del heno	febbre da fieno
cabeza	testa
dolor de cobexe	mal di testa
corazon	cuore
hospital	ospedale
calor	caldo
seguro	assicurazione
medusa	medusa
rodilla	ginocchio
humedecedora	umidificatore
dinero	soldi
mosquito	zanzara
boca	bocca

English	Francais
Neck	cou
Nose	nez
Pain	douleur
Poison	poison
Scald	brûlure
Sick (unwell)	malade
Soap	savon
Sprain	entorse
Sticking plaster	sparadrap
Sunburn	hâle
Suntan Lotion	crème à bronzer
Throat	gorge
Tooth	dent
Toothache	mal des dents
Toothbrush	brosse á dent
Toothpaste	pâte dentifrice
Unconscious	sans connaisance
Wasp	guêpe
Water	eau
Wrist	poignet

Espanol	Italiano
quello	colle
nariz	naso
dolor	dolore
veneno	veleno
quemadura	scottatura
enfermo	malato
jabon	sapone
torcido	storta
esparadrapo	cerotti
quemaduras del sol	bruciatura da sole
crema del sol	lozione per abbronzatura
garganta	gola
muelas	dente
dolor de muelas	mal di denti
cepillo de dientes	spazzolino da denti
pasta de dientes	dentifricio
inconsió	inconscio
vespa	vespa
aqua	acqua
muneca	polso

METRIC CONVERSION TABLES

Everybody needs time to adjust to the weights and measures used on the continent. The most common difficulty is with lbs and kgs and litres and pints.

Probably the three most useful figures to remember are:

1 Kg is **2 1/5 lbs; 1 litre** is just over **1¾ pints; 1 gallon** is just over **4½ litres.**

So if you want to buy 1 lb of apples, ask for ½ a kilo, and if you want 1 pint of beer, ask for ½ a litre.

TEMPERATURE

● Average normal human body temperature in metric is 37°C

°C	35	36	37	38	39	40	41	42

°F 95 96 97 98 99 100   102   104   106   108

WEIGHT

1 oz is 28.349 grams. For practical weighing, 1 oz is taken as 25 grams for amounts under 1 lb, and 30 grams for amounts over 1 lb.

1 oz	4 oz	8 oz	1 lb	2 lb
25g	100g	200g	450g	900g

VOLUME

1 pint is 568.26 millilitres (ml).
Below are rough equivalents.

¼ pint	½ pint	1 pint	2 pints
150 ml	300 ml	600 ml	1200 ml

LENGTH

1 metre (m) is 39.37 inches. Approximate measurements are:

1"	1 yd	39"	1 mile	0.6 mile
25mm	0.9m	1m	1.6 Km	1 Km

MOTORING

Tyre pressures, as well as petrol pumps, have also come in for metrication. The following two tables show rough equivalents.

Petrol measures		Tyre pressures	
litres	gallons	lb/sq in	kg/cm^2
5	1.1	10	0.7
10	2.2	15	1.1
15	3.3	18	1.3
20	4.4	21	1.5
25	5.5	23	1.6
30	6.6	26	1.8
35	7.7	28	2.0
40	8.8	30	2.1
45	9.9	36	2.5
50	11.0	38	2.7
		40	2.8

CLOTHING SIZES (Approximate)

Women's Dresses and Suits

British:	8	10	12	14	16	18
Continental:	–	38	40	42	44	46

Women's Shoes

British:	4½	5	5½	6	6½	7
Continental:	38	38	39	39	40	41

Men's Shirts

British:	14	14½	15	15½	16	17
Continental:	36	37	38	39/40	41	43

Men's Shoes

British:	7½	8½	9½	10½	11½
Continental:	42	43	44	45	46

WORLD STANDARD TIMES

Accra	GMT	Cape Town	1400 (+ 2)
Amsterdam	1300 (+ 1)	Caracas	0800 (− 4)
Ankara	1400 (+ 2)	Chicago	0600 (− 6)
Athens	1400 (+ 2)	Copenhagen	1300 (+ 1)
Auckland	2400 (+ 12)	Dar-es-Salaam	1500 (+ 3)
Baghdad	1500 (+ 3)	Darwin	2130 (+ 9½)
Bangkok	1900 (+ 7)	Delhi	1700 (+ 5)
Belgrade	1300 (+ 1)	Dublin	GMT
Berne	1300 (+ 1)	Helsinki	1400 (+ 2)
Bogota	0700 (− 5)	Hong Kong	2000 (+ 8)
Bombay	1730 (+ 5½)	Jerusalem	1400 (+ 2)
Bonn	1300 (+ 1)	Johannesburg	1400 (+ 2)
Brasilia	0900 (− 3)	Karachi	1700 (+ 5)
Brussels	1300 (+ 1)	Kuala Lumpur	2000 (+ 8)
Buenos Aires	0900 (− 3)	Kuwait	1500 (+ 3)
Cairo	1400 (+ 2)	Lagos	1300 (+ 1)
Calcutta	1730 (+ 5½)	Lisbon	GMT

These times are based on + or − Greenwich Mean Time (GMT).
British Summer Time (BST) commences March 25, 1984.
Note: This map is schematic and times are approximate only.

London	GMT	Riyadh	1500 (+ 3)
Los Angeles	0400 (− 8)	Rome	1300 (+ 1)
Madrid	1300 (+ 1)	San Francisco	0400 (− 8)
Mexico City	0600 (− 6)	Seoul	2100 (+ 9)
Montreal	0700 (− 5)	Singapore	2000 (+ 8)
Moscow	1500 (+ 3)	Stockholm	1300 (+ 1)
Muscat	1600 (+ 4)	Sydney	2200 (+ 10)
Nairobi	1500 (+ 3)	Tokyo	2100 (+ 9)
New York	0700 (− 5)	Tripoli	1400 (+ 2)
Oslo	1300 (+ 1)	Vancouver	0400 (− 8)
Ottawa	0700 (− 5)	Vienna	1300 (+ 1)
Paris	1300 (+ 1)	Vladivostock	2200 (+ 10)
Peking	2000 (+ 8)	Warsaw	1300 (+ 1)
Perth	2000 (+ 8)	Washington	0700 (− 5)
Pretoria	1400 (+ 2)	Wellington	2400 (+ 12)
Quebec	0700 (− 5)		
Rio de Janeiro	0900 (− 3)		

'PHONE HOME!
IT'S AS EASY AS STD

To dial the United Kingdom from abroad, dial the access code to the International Equipment. This differs from country to country. Then dial the UK country code which is always **44,** followed by the full UK national number **excluding** the STD access digit **'0'.**

If the STD code you dial changes from different parts of the country, ask the operator which code to use from overseas, before you go.

Examples

1. To call Aberdeen (STD code 0224) 12345 from GREECE, dial 00 44 224 12345. Dial steadily without long pauses between the digits.

2. To call Leeds (STD code 0532) 56789 from HONG KONG, dial 106 44 532 56789.

All the countries from which you can dial direct
to the UK are listed in the following table, correct
at December 1983.
Please note that the service may not be available
from everywhere in the countries listed below.

COUNTRY	ACCESS DIGITS	COMMENTS
Algeria	00 44	
Andorra	0 44	– After '0' await high pitched tone before continuing.
Antilles (Neth)	00 44	
Argentina	00 44	
Australia	0011 44	
Austria	00 44	
Bahamas	011 44	
Bahrain	00 44	
Barbados	NK	(Not known)
Belgium	00 44	– After '00' await second dialling tone before continuing.
Bermuda	1 44	
Brazil	00 44	
Brunei	00 44	
Cameroon	00 44	
Canada	011 44	
Cayman Is	0 44	
Costa Rica	00 44	
Cyprus	00 44	
Czechoslovakia	00 44	
Denmark	009 44	
Egypt	00 44	
Finland	990 44	
France	19 44	– After '19' await high pitched tone before continuing.
Gabon	NK	
German Dem. Rep.	012 44	
Germany Fed. Rep.	00 44	
Gibraltar	00 44	
Greece	00 44	
Guatemala	00 44	
Hong Kong	106 44	
Hungary	00 44	

Iceland	90 44	
India	900 44	
Indonesia	00 44	
Iran	00 44	
Iraq	00 44	
Israel	00 44	
Italy	00 44	
Ivory Coast	00 44	
Japan	001 44	
Jordan	0, 00 or 13 44 –	00 and 13 to be replaced by 0 in the near future.
Kuwait	00 44	
Lebanon	00 44	
Liechtenstein	00 44	
Luxembourg	00 44	
Macao	00 44	
Malawi	101 44	
Malaysia	00 44	
Malta	0 44	
Mexico	00 44	
Monaco	19 44 –	After '19' await high pitched tone before continuing.
Morocco	00 44	
Namibia	091 44	
Netherlands	09 44 –	After '09' await second dialling tone before continuing.
New Zealand	00 44	
Nigeria	009 44	
Norway	095 44	
Oman	00 44	
Pakistan	00 44	
Papua New Guinea	31 44	
Panama	00 44	
Philippines	00 44	
Poland	00 44	
Portugal	07 44	
Qatar	00 44	
San Marino	00 44	
Saudi Arabia	00 44	
Senegal	00 44	
Singapore	005 44	

South Africa	091 44	
South Korea	001 44	
Spain	07 44	– After '07' await high pitched tone before continuing.
Sri Lanka	00 44	
Surinam	001 44	
Swaziland	00 44	
Sweden	009 44	– A second dialling tone is received after 009 44.
Switzerland	00 44	
Syria	00 44	
Taiwan	002 44	
Trinidad & Tobago	01 44	
Tunisia	00 44	
Turkey	99 44	– A second dialling tone is received after the initial 9.
United Arab Emirates (Abu Dhabi, Fujairah, Ras Al Khaimah)	00 44	
(Ajman, Dubai, Umm Al Qaiwan)	010 44	
(Sharjah)	000 44	
Uruguay	00 44	
USA	011 44	– After dialling '0' dial the second digit within 7 seconds otherwise a USA local operator will come into the line.
USSR	810 44	
Venezuela	00 44	
Yemen Arab Rep.	00 44	
Yugoslavia	99 44	

Source: British Telecom.

The following list, reproduced by permission of the DHSS, shows for each country in the world:

R = Vaccinations or tablets recommended for protection against disease.
E = Vaccinations which are an essential requirement for entry to the country concerned and for which you will require a certificate.

The list is correct at the time of print (January 1984) for journeys **direct from Britain.** For journeys to more than one country, or for any changes, check before you go.

Country	Cholera	Malaria	Typhoid	Polio	Yellow Fever
Afghanistan	R	R	R	R	
Albania			R		
Algeria	R	R	R	R	
Angola	R	R	R	R	R
Antilles, Neth.			R	R	
Argentina		R	R	R	
Australia					
Austria					
Azores			R	R	
Bahamas			R	R	
Bahrain	R		R	R	
Bangladesh	R	R	R	R	
Barbados			R	R	
Belgium					
Belize		R	R	R	
Benin	R	R	R	R	E – except children under 1 year old
Bermuda					
Bhutan	R	R	R	R	
Bolivia		R	R	R	E – if going to Santa Cruz de la Sierra
Botswana	R	R	R	R	
Brazil		R	R	R	R – except children under 1 year old
Brunei	R		R	R	

85

Country	Cholera	Malaria	Typhoid	Polio	Yellow Fever
Bulgaria			R		
Burma	R	R	R	R	
Burundi	R	R	R	R	R – except children under 1 year old
Cameroon	R	R	R	R	E – except children under 1 year old
Canada					
Canal Zone, Panama		R	R	R	
Canary Islands			R	R	
Cape Verde Islands		R	R	R	
Cayman Islands			R	R	
Central African Republic	R	R	R	R	E – except children under 1 year old
Chad	R	R	R	R	R – except children under 1 year old
Chile			R	R	
China		R	R	R	
Colombia		R	R	R	R – except children under 1 year old
Comoros		R	R	R	
Congo	R	R	R	R	E – except travellers arriving from a non-infected area and staying less than 2 weeks; and children under 1 year old.

Country	Cholera	Malaria	Typhoid	Polio	Yellow Fever
Cook Islands			R	R	
Costa Rica		R	R	R	
Cuba			R	R	
Cyprus			R		
Czechoslovakia					
Denmark					
Djibouti	R	R	R	R	
Dominica			R	R	
Dominican Rep.		R	R	R	
Ecuador		R	R	R	R – except children under 1 year old
Egypt	R	R	R	R	
El Salvador		R	R	R	
Equatorial Guinea	R	R	R	R	R – except children under 1 year old
Ethiopia	R	R	R	R	R – except children under 1 year old
Falkland Islands			R	R	
Fiju			R	R	
Finland					
France			R		Mediterranean coastal area only
Gabon	R	R	R	R	R – except children under 1 year old
Gambia	R	R	R	R	E – except children under 1 year old

87

Country	Cholera	Malaria	Typhoid	Polio	Yellow Fever
German Dem. Rep. (East)					
German Fed. Rep. (West)					
Ghana	R	R	R	R	R – except children under 1 year old
Gibraltar			R		
Greece			R		
Greenland					
Grenada			R	R	
Guam			R	R	
Guatemala		R	R	R	
Guiana, French		R	R	R	E – except travellers arriving from a non-infected area and staying less than 2 weeks and children under 1 year old
Guinea	R	R	R	R	R – except children under 1 year old
Guinea Bissau	R	R	R	R	R – except children under 1 year old
Guyana		R	R	R	R – except children under 1 year old
Haiti		R	R	R	
Honduras		R	R	R	
Hong Kong			R	R	

Country	Cholera	Malaria	Typhoid	Polio	Yellow Fever
Hungary					
Iceland					
India	R	R	R	R	
Indonesia	R	R	R	R	
Iran	R	R	R	R	
Iraq	R	R	R	R	
Irish Republic					
Israel	R		R	R	
Italy			R		
Ivory Coast	R	R	R	R	E – except children under 1 year old
Jamaica			R	R	
Japan			R	R	
Jordan	R	R	R	R	
Kampuchea	R	R	R	R	
Kenya	R	R	R	R	R – except children under 1 year old
Kiribati			R	R	
Korea (North)	R		R	R	
Korea (South)	R	R	R	R	
Kuwait	R		R	R	
Laos (Lao)	R	R	R	R	
Lebanon	R		R	R	
Lesotho	R		R	R	
Liberia	R	R	R	R	R – except children under 1 year old

Country	Cholera	Malaria	Typhoid	Polio	Yellow Fever
Libya	R	R	R	R	
Luxembourg					
Madagascar	R	R	R	R	
Madeira			R	R	
Malawi	R	R	R	R	
Malaysia	R	R	R	R	
Maldives	R	R	R	R	
Mali	R	R	R	R	E – except travellers arriving from a non-infected area and staying less than 2 weeks
Malta			R		
Mauritania	R	R	R	R	E – except travellers arriving from a non-infected area and staying less than 2 weeks; and children under 1 year old.
Mauritius		R	R		
Mexico		R	R	R	
Monaco			R		
Mongolia			R	R	
Montserrat			R	R	
Morocco	R	R	R	R	
Mozambique	E	R	R	R	
Namibia	R	R	R	R	

Country	Cholera	Malaria	Typhoid	Polio	Yellow Fever
Nauru			R	R	
Nepal	R	R	R	R	
Netherlands					
New Caledonia			R	R	
New Zealand					
Nicaragua		R	R	R	
Niger	R	R	R	R	E – except children under 1 year old
Nigeria	R	R	R	R	E – except children under 1 year old
Niue			R	R	
Norway					
Oman	R	R	R	R	
Pakistan	R	R	R	R	
Panama			R	R	R – except children under 1 year old
Papua New Guinea	R	R	R	R	
Paraguay		R	R	R	
Peru		R	R	R	R – except children under 1 year old
Philippines	R	R	R	R	
Pitcairn Island			R	R	
Poland					
Polynesia,French			R	R	
Portugal			R		

Country	Cholera	Malaria	Typhoid	Polio	Yellow Fever
Puerto Rico			R	R	
Qatar	R	R	R	R	
Reunion Islands			R		
Romania			R		
Rwanda	R	R	R	R	R – except children under 1 year old
Saint Helena			R	R	
Saint Lucia			R	R	
Saint Vincent and Grenadines			R	R	
Somoa			R	R	
Sao Tome and Principe	R	R	R	R	E – except travellers coming from a non-infected area and staying less than 2 weeks; and children under 1 year old
Saudi Arabia	R	R	R	R	
Senegal	R	R	R	R	E – except children under 1 year old
Seychelles			R	R	
Sierra Leone	R	R	R	R	R – except children under 1 year old. A certificate may be required on leaving the country.
Singapore	R		R	R	
Solomon Islands		R	R	R	

Country	Cholera	Malaria	Typhoid	Polio	Yellow Fever
Somalia	R	R	R	R	R – except children under 1 year old
South Africa	R	R	R	R	
Spain			R		
Sri Lanka	R	R	R	R	
Sudan	R	R	R	R	R – except children under 1 year old. A certificate may be required on leaving the country.
Surinam		R	R	R	R – except children under 1 year old
Swaziland	R	R	R	R	
Sweden					
Switzerland					
Syria	R	R	R	R	
Taiwan	R		R	R	
Tanzania	R	R	R	R	R – except children under 1 year old
Thailand	R	R	R	R	
Timor, East	R	R	R	R	
Togo	R	R	R	R	R – except children under 1 year old
Trinidad and Tobago			R	R	
Tunisia	R		R	R	
Turkey	R	R	R	R	
Tuvalu			R	R	

Country	Cholera	Malaria	Typhoid	Polio	Yellow Fever
Uganda	R	R	R	R	E – except children under 1 year old
United Arab Emirates	R	R	R	R	
USA					
USSR			R		
Upper Volta	R	R	R	R	E – except children under 1 year old
Uruguay			R	R	
Vanuatu		R	R	R	
Venezuela		R	R	R	R – except children under 1 year old
Vietnam	R	R	R	R	
Virgin Islands			R	R	
West Indies Assoc. States			R	R	
French West Indies			R	R	
Yemen Dem. Rep. (South)	R	R	R	R	
Yemen Arab Rep. (North)	R	R	R	R	
Yugoslavia			R		
Zaire	R	R	R	R	R – except children under 1 year old
Zambia	R	R	R	R	R – except children under 1 year old
Zimbabwe	R	R	R	R	

NOTES